How to personalize this book for your Dear Grandson

Original cover

Tools needed: (all are available at a scrapbook supply store and/or craft store)

- Acid-free glue stick
- Photo mounting squares/tape
- Scissors or photo trimmer
- Fine point writing pen (acid-free, light-fast, waterproof, fade-proof, smear-proof and non-bleeding)
- Acid-free paper for writing additional notes/letters

Dear Friends,

As a grandparent, you have the precious gifts of history to share with your grandson — memories of your own life plus wisdom and dreams for his. Using our book as your 'canvas,' you can embellish as much or as little as you wish, creating a keepsake your grandson will cherish forever. Some ways to personalize:

Customize the cover photo

Slip out the cover insert and paste your special photo in the indicated area.

Cover personalized with photo

Affix your photos over ours!

One of the easiest ways to make this book your own is to gather your favorite photos and adhere them over the ones we show. Some spaces are a traditional 4 x 6 size; others are circular or sub-sized. For the cleanest cuts, you would want to use a photo trimmer (see above).

Page personalized with photo and journaling

Record "guided" memories

With our guided journal pages, you can share fond
memories from a time your grandson will never know.
Perhaps he will discover much in common
with his grandmother!

Page personalized with photo and journaling

Share your wisdom

What words of wisdom would you like to share with
your grandson? You can certainly add your anecdotes
to any page. We have, however, built in a special page for
grandmother's wisdom.

Page personalized with memento (fortune) and journaling

Capture the spirit of your grandson

Do you see in your grandchild a budding musician?
Is he a book or animal lover? Celebrate how you see him
by creating a page about him with photos, mementos,
and musings.

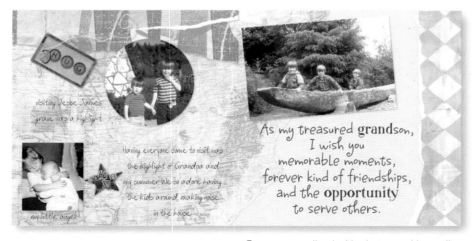

Page personalized with photos and journaling

Dear Grandson

a message of Love

by Marianne Richmond

Dear Grandson
a message of Love

Library of Congress Control Number: 2007903347

A special thanks to the creative companies whose papers we incorporated into our designs: daisyd's, Karen Foster Design, Design Originials, Making Memories©, K&Company LLC, C.R. Gibson, Masterpiece Studios.

Marianne Richmond Studios, Inc.
3900 Stinson Boulevard NE
Minneapolis, MN 55421
www.mariannerichmond.com

ISBN 10: 1-934082-02-3
ISBN 13: 978-1-934082-02-7

Illustrations by Marianne Richmond

Book design by Sara Dare Biscan

Printed in China

First Printing

This book is dedicated to beloved grandsons everywhere, especially Cole, Adam, Will, and Jacob. — MR

A gifted author and illustrator, Marianne Richmond lives in Minneapolis, MN with her husband, four children and one dog.

Marianne shares her unique spirit and enchanting artwork in her other titles:

The Gift of an Angel
The Gift of a Memory
Hooray for You!,
The Gifts of Being Grand
I Love You So...
Dear Daughter
Dear Son
Dear Granddaughter
My Shoes Take Me Where I Want to Go
Fish Kisses and Gorilla Hugs

Marianne continues to create products that help people connect with those who mean the most to them. Her repertoire includes books, stationery and giftware.

www.mariannerichmond.com

Pages are acid and lignin free

Dear _____

_____

_____

_____

_____

Love,

_____

Nobody can do for children what grandparents do. Grandparents sort of sprinkle stardust over the lives of children. —Alex Haley

DEAR

Grandson,

You **truly** are a dear grandson.

1 2 MADE IN U.S.A. 3

Adored
beyond measure.

How

Blessed

I am to have
the gift of you
in my Life.

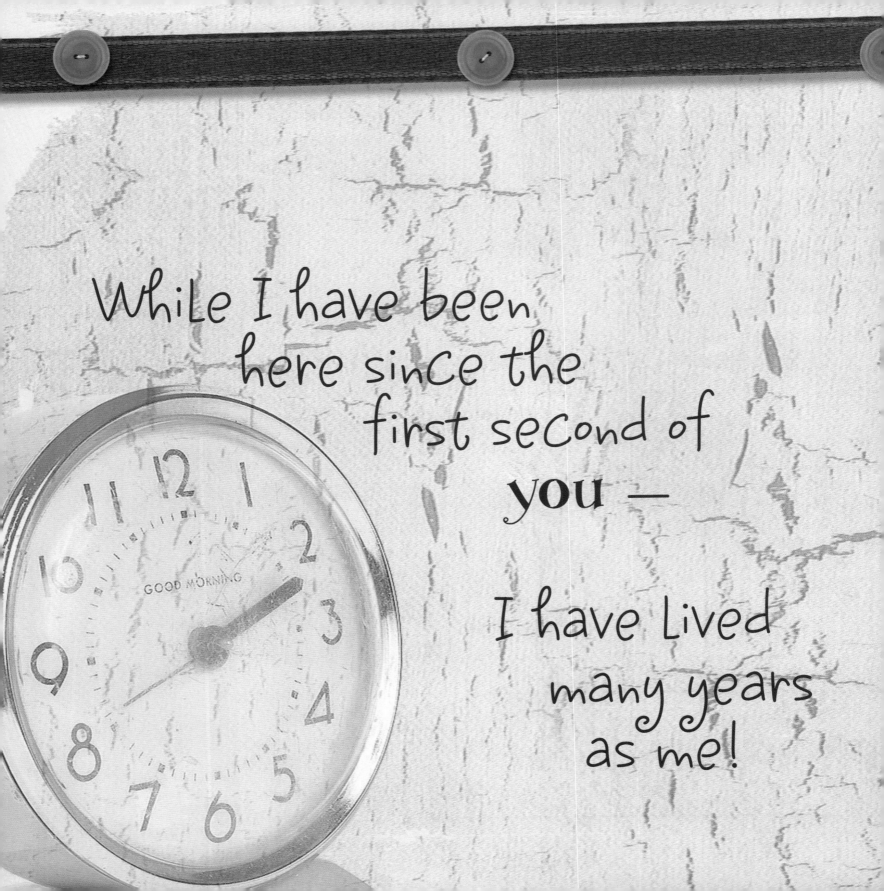

WELCOME TO MINNESOTA

...ARTMENT OF HIGHWAYS

Can you imagine your grandmother as a baby? A teenager? Or as a young bride?

There are a few things I'd like to share with you about **my life**, just in case you ever find yourself wishing you knew.

Certificate of Birth

My full name

That name was chosen because

I weighed

I was born

weight

date

length

My parents names

Brothers and sisters

My family lived on this street

in this town

I remember my neighborhood as...

As a young girl...

My chores included

I went to school at

My favorite things to do with my friends were

Some of my favorite things were

Sports

Foods

Colors

School Subjects

Friends

And as a young Lady...

I graduated in   from

After I finished school, I

My first job was

I began to date at the age of

I met your grandfather at

we went on dates to

I was   years old
and he was

We were married on

I liked him because

in the year of

I remember the
first time I held you,
and the **instant**,
all Consuming,

giGanTiC

love I felt.

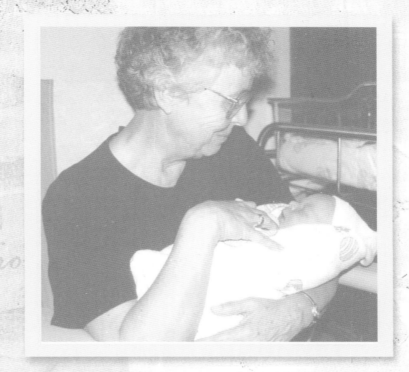

I celebrated your every accomplishment, big and small.

As I watch **you** grow,
I am in awe of the
remarkably **charming** young man
you are.

Time after time,
you touch my heart
with your affection,
your playfulness,
and your extraordinary
individuality.

The things I **especially** appreciate about you are:

I love being your **grand** mother, because my job is great joy — loving you, spoiling you, hanging out with you... and encouraging you.

(I can happily leave the discipline stuff up to your parents!)

My favorite moments
with you are...

SPECIAL MOMENTS

In my life,
I have always loved to...

DREAM BIG DREAMS
BELIEVE
THEY'LL COME TRUE

and
have felt
passionate
about...

In your journey through Life, I want you to discover exactly who **you** are — your talents, your passions, your goals and your dreams...

that appears at regular inter...
...nunc *journal* >
syn magazine, newspaper, organ, periodical, review
journey *n* passing or a passage from one place to another
  <at that time it was a four day *journey* from Boston to
  New York> <she was tired though their *journey* was barely
  begun>
  syn expedition, peregrination(s), travel(s), trek, trip; *com-*
  pare TRIP 1
  rel excursion, jaunt, junket, sally, tour; cruise, voyage;
  pilgrimage, progress, safari
journey *vb* **syn** GO 1, fare, hie, pass, proceed, ||process
  push on, repair, travel, wend
jovial *adj* **syn** MERRY blit... blithesome, festive, gay,

JOURNEY

AND to have the

CHANCE to design

A life

that

Celebrates

your

WONDERFUL

un**i**queness!

As my treasured **grandson**,
I wish you
memorable moments,
forever kind of friendships,
and the **opportunity**
to serve others.

Believe it or not, I was young once, too.

I went through "**phases**." Made poor choices. Had my heart broken and my feelings hurt. Disappointed my parents. Let down a friend.

I survived and (usually) learned from my experiences.

How else could I gain my grandmotherly wisdom?

If I may offer some of
   this "hard-won guidance,"
I'd tuck a few gems
   in your heart...

Forgive... even if you
               can't forget.

Be honest,
     even if it's tough to do.

Walk away when you feel like saying or doing something you might regret.

Imagine yourself in another's shoes to gain understanding.

Oh, and a couple other thoughts...

I wish I could **guarantee** you a trouble-free trip through life. But, grandmothers don't fib.

What I can tell you, however, is that struggles make you stronger, smarter, and more sensitive to others.

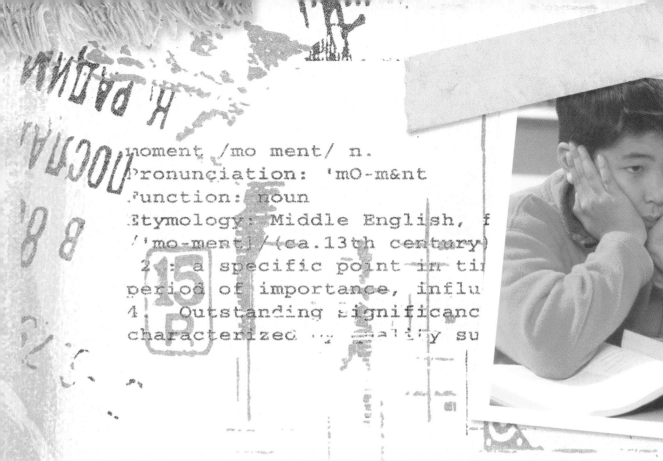

moment /mo ment/ n.
Pronunciation: 'mO-m&nt
Function: noun
Etymology: Middle English, f   Latin
/'mo-mentl/ (ca.13th century)   ite inte
2 : a specific point in ti   t time
period of importance, influ   a serie
4 : Outstanding significanc   events
characterized   ality su   bility o

They also make you welcome
joy with outstretched arms —
and a thankful heart.

And this is all good.

You know the saying about misfortune being a

"blessing in disguise"...

It can be true, I promise....

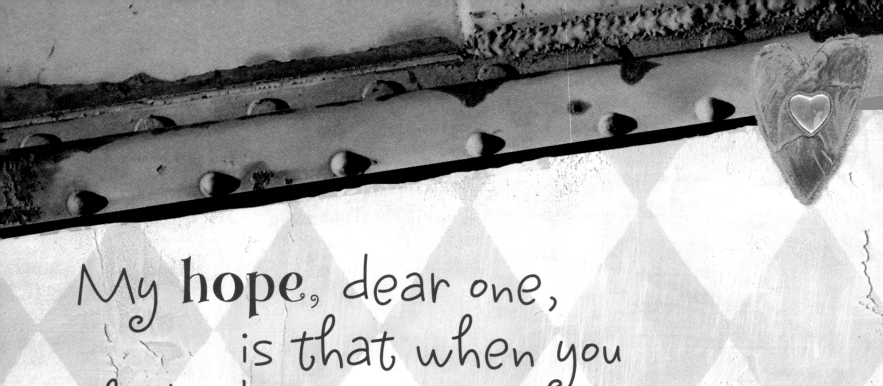

My **hope**, dear one,
        is that when you
think about your
        grandmother,
        it is with

INSPIRE

HOPE   GROW

PrIDe

Love

and

A D

M I R

A T I O N

as I do about
you,
my dear,

dear
grandson.